The Traveller's From The Sky
A children's short story with pictures

Semisi Pule

Copyright © Rainbow Enterprises 2015

Publisher: Rainbow Enterprises 2015

ISBN: 978-1-98-851162-7

All rights reserved. No part of this publication shall be reproduced without prior written consent from the publisher and copyright holder. Rainbow Enterprises is the trade/publisher name of Semisi Pule aka Semisi Pule Pone.

Distribution by Rainbow Enterprises.

Email: rainbowenterprises7@gmail.com

Note: This story has been published before as part of the novel 'The Children of the Gods. The combined Trilogy' (amazon.com). All art work for this book was done by the author.

THE BEGINNING

A long time ago, during the age of magic, demons and gods, during the rule of the Tu'i Tonga Empire in the

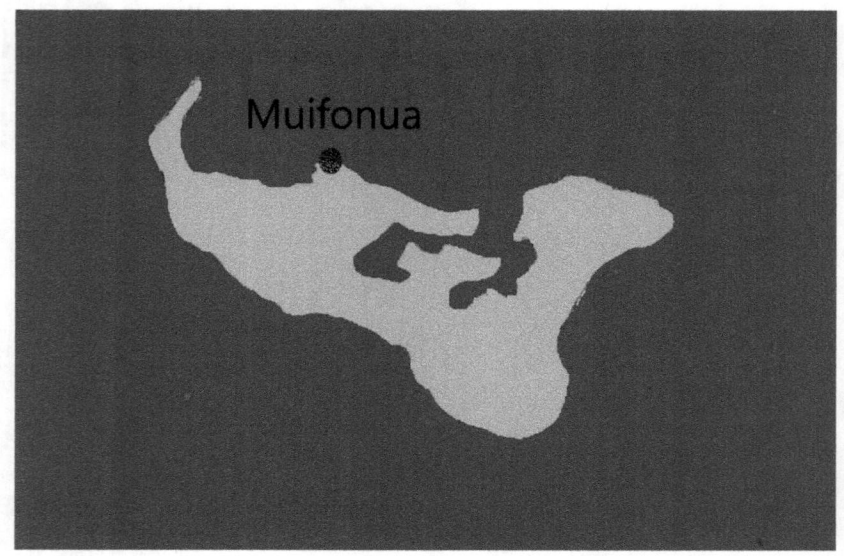

South Pacific, there lived a couple on the beach at Muifonua. It was the western tip of a piece of land that

jutted out from the central seafront of Tongatapu, the sacred island of the Tuʻi Tonga Empire.

Mafanga, the wife, had long silky black hair that ended at

her waistline and clear, fair skin. She was a very beautiful woman.

Mafanga was always busy making mats and tapa, a traditional Polynesian cloth which she used to craft clothes and blankets. Her husband Latou was tall, toned and handsome and had a rich brown tan from all the outdoor work. He was a farmer and grew crops inland, such as yams, taro and

Latou's garden

plantain. He was also a very

good fisherman. Latou

specialized in catching mullet with
his net, especially during the breeding season when the mullet migrated from the lagoon to Muifonua. Mullet

was Mafanga's favourite food, alongside roasted yams.

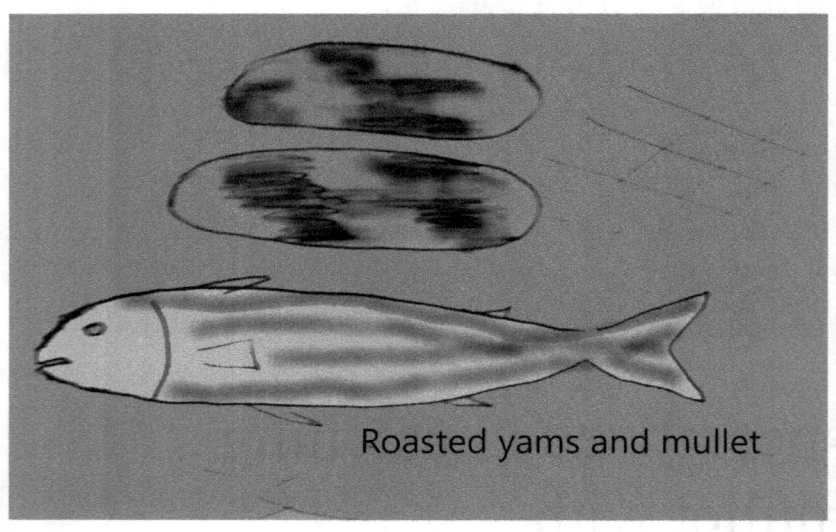
Roasted yams and mullet

Latou and Mafanga lived happily, though they were

always hopeful they would have children.

After several years with no children, Mafanga had an idea.

   "Perhaps if you gave Niutahi some of your fish, he might grant us children," Mafanga suggested. "He is, after all, the most powerful God in this area."

Latou throwing the fattest mullet into the sea

Latou nodded in agreement. "Sounds like a good idea. I'll throw the fattest mullet I catch into the sea every day as a sacrifice to Niutahi so that he may grant our wish."

Latou threw the fattest mullet into the sea every day for 6 months, but nothing happened.

Latou throws two fattest mullets into the sea

Mafanga was still hopeful. She asked Latou to try throwing the 2 fattest mullets into the sea; maybe that would work. Latou agreed and did so, but after another 6 months there was still no success.

THE STORM

One day, Latou went fishing in his canoe and was caught in a violent storm. The waves thrashed his canoe and threatened to overturn it as the wind pounded his sails and blew him further out to sea. The sky was painted black with ominous rain clouds.

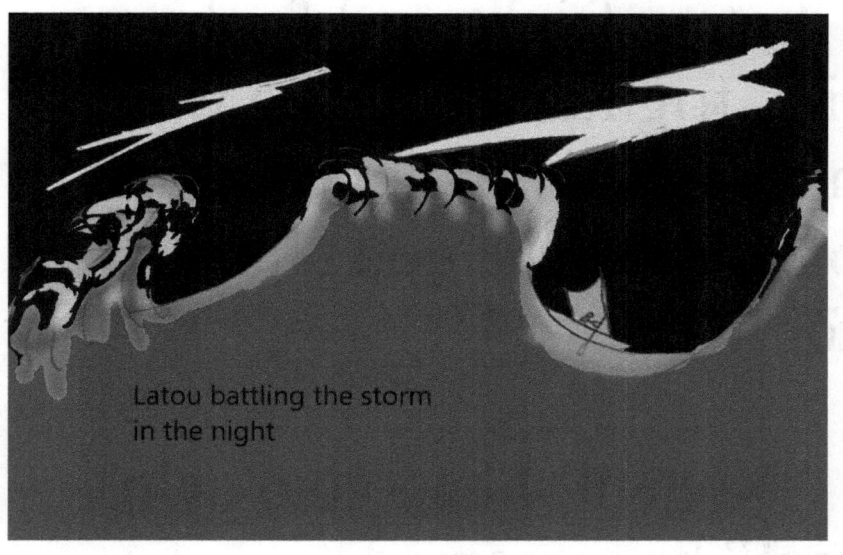

Latou battling the storm in the night

Lightning struck every now and then, filling the world with light for a split second before the darkness returned. The noise of the howling wind was deafening.

Latou, frightened for his life, frightened that he would never see his beloved again, pleaded to the god Niutahi for help.

"Niutahi! I beg you, help me!" he screamed.

Thunder cracked across the sky, drowning out his cries for help.

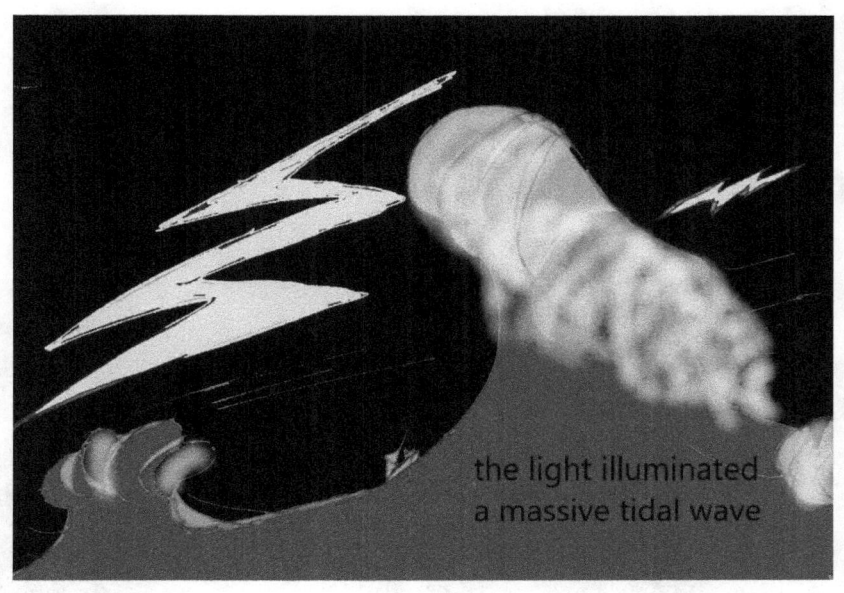

the light illuminated a massive tidal wave

The light illuminated a massive tidal wave that just caught Latou's eye before it came crashing down on his canoe, forcing it under the water. Latou held on for dear life, coughing up water when he surfaced. Afraid that he might fall

Latou saw a triangular sail on the horizon

off the canoe, he tied himself down with some coconut rope.

Latou was beginning to lose consciousness. He lay on his canoe, cold and wet as the rain beat down on him. He thinks of his lovely wife and their warm house, it keeps him determined to get back to her.

'ETUMATUPU'A

Latou woke up, the light and heat of the midday sun forcing his eyes to squint. The sea was calm, but the gentle rocking of the canoe remind him of the storm. The mast and the sail were gone. Probably taken by the huge wave, he thought. He was lucky the outriggers were still tied together.

Latou searched the horizon for land or birds when a triangular sail caught his eye from far off in the distance.

As time passed, the triangular sail came closer and closer, so Latou lay on the deck and shouted for help. His voice was hoarse from his pleads of help the night before, and his throat was dry from the seawater he had swallowed. Eventually, he passed out again.

The sounds of shouting coaxed Latou's eyes open. He used the remainder of what little strength he had left to sit up. In front of him,

The kalia loomed over him like a great wall

just a few metres away was

the kalia that he had seen in the distance. It loomed over him like a great wall. People with head dresses of colorful feathers stared at him from the deck worriedly.

"Help," Latou whispered weakly. He had no strength left; the storm had broken his spirit.

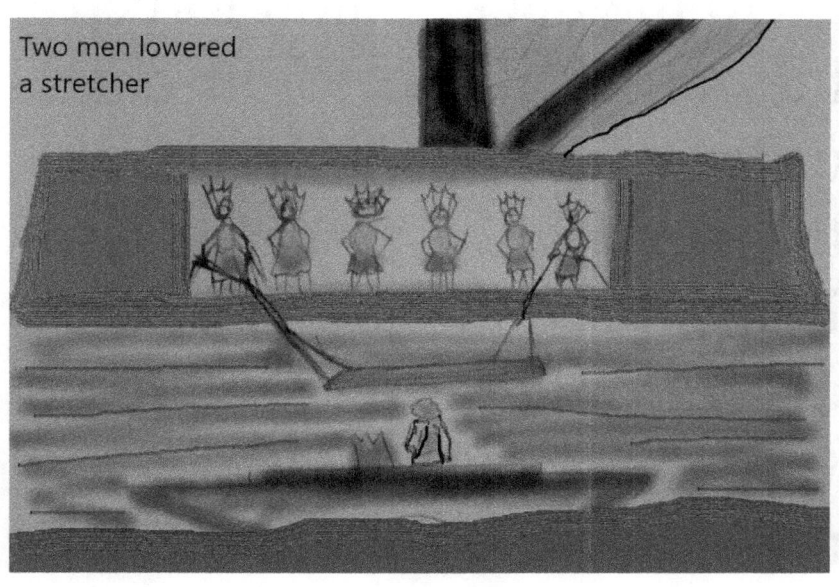

Two men lowered a stretcher

The kalia came closer and two men lowered themselves onto his canoe with a stretcher made of hibiscus bark rope. They tied him to the stretcher and pulled him up to the deck. Latou forced himself on his feet. In front of him, sat upon a wooden throne, was a titan of a man. Latou was tall but the man sitting in front of him was at least a foot taller. His muscles were prominent under his traditional Polynesian garb. He held in his right hand an ironwood club that he wielded like a sceptre. Behind him he could see the kalia lanterns lit up from inside. Several warriors stood beside him with long ironwood spears. It was

In front of him upon a throne sat a titan of a man

clear to Latou that this man was the chief.

The man thudded his club on the floor twice and the crowd went silent. Latou kneeled out of respect.

"I am 'Etumatupu'a", the man said in a deep, booming voice.

"My kalia is called Lele-i-Matangi."

'Etumatupu'a gestured towards the crowd. "I sailed from Samoa to return my relatives from Mu'a to Upolu. They came to bring their first yam harvest for the Tu'i Tonga."

Latou bowed his head.

"Thank you for your kindness 'Etumatupu'a. My name is Latou and I am from Muifonua. I went fishing and I was caught in a wild storm. I almost lost my life and I thought all hope was lost until you found me."

Latou looked at 'Etumatupu'a, who gestured at him to stand.

"My wife Mafanga is waiting for me at home. If I had some fish left, I would give them all to you, but I sacrificed them all to Niutahi so that he might grant us children."

Latou went on to explain his sacrifices to Niutahi in the past year with no success.

'Etumatupu'a, moved by Latou's story, offered to help him.

"Wake up early each morning and check the rising sun," 'Etumatupu'a explained. "If the sky is clear for 3 days in a row, prepare a sleep house for 4 people. Some visitors will come and stay with you for one month. After they leave, Mafanga will become pregnant every year for 4 years. She will bear 4 children. I ask only of you that you name them 'Etu, Ma, Tupu'a and Langi."

Latou agreed to his offer without a second thought, then 'Etumatupu'a took Latou to Muifonua and continued on his voyage to Mu'a.

After several weeks of rainy weather, the sky cleared for 3 days. Latou, remembering 'Etumatupu'a's advice, prepared a sleep house made of coconut fronds and

Latou prepared a sleephouse made of coconut fronds

mangrove wood.

One morning, a large shadow cast over Muifonua. Latou ran to see what was obscuring the sunlight and

One morning a large shadow cast over Muifonua

his eyes were just able to make out the outline of the sails of a massive Kalia approaching from the east.

When the Kalia finally got close enough to anchor and Latou was able to appreciate its true size, four beings that looked like children, emerged from the ocean,

Four beings that look like children emerged

walking on to the land. The seawater slid off their skin and clothes, leaving it clean and dry. They all looked the same, with all of them sporting clean shaven heads and eyes that glowed like the

sunrise. Their white garments as white as the foaming wave tops.
Every morning the four children would stand on the beach with their hands raised towards the rising sun.

Every morning the four children would stand on the beach

At noon they would retreat into their sleep house that Latou had built and sleep all day until the next morning, where the ritual would repeat. Occasionally, Latou offered them food and drink, but they simply waved it away. After a while he took the initiative and stopped offering.

After one month, Latou woke up to find the Kalia and the children have gone.

In the 30 days that they had spent at his home, he had not heard them utter a single word.

As 'Etumatupu'a predicted, Mafanga became pregnant for 4 years in a row. She bore 3 sons and 1 daughter. Latou and Mafanga abided by 'Etumatupu'a's wish and named the boys 'Etu, Ma and Tupu'a. They also named the daughter Langi.

Latou also named their place at Muifonua "Laku-ika-fua-'i-Moana", which means "Sacrifices that bore fruit from the deep."

Latou and Mafanga were happier then they had ever been in a long time. Raising their children together was their dream come true granted by 'Etumatupu'a, the God he met in the ocean.

…..THE END….

The Dreamtime Stories

These dreamtime stories are also available from Rainbow Enterprises Books and amazon.com.

1. The Prince and the Governor's Daughter
2. Aris and the Taniwha
3. Aris and the Spaceship
4. The Magic Mountain
5. Banana Bunch
6. The Feijoa Tree
7. The Travelling Merchant
8. Pawns in other People's Games
9. Alana and Kiteni's Holiday
10. The Mermaids of Hawaiki
11. The Romance
12. The Rugby Game
13. Mic and the Sea Goddess

Questions.

Test the children's recall of the story by asking these questions and look for the answers, in the story, together.

1. What are the names of the couple that lived at Muifonua?.
2. What is the name of the scared island of the Tu'i Tonga Empire?
3. What crops did Latou grew inland?
4. What kind of fish Latou specialized in catching?
5. How did Latou catch the fish?
6. How many fish did he throw in the sea?
7. Why did he throw the fish in the sea?
8. What is Mafanga's favorite food?
9. Who was the God that Latou met at sea?
10. Did the Gods send the storm to blow him into 'Etumatupu'a's path?
11. What did 'Etumatupu'a promise Latou?
12. How many children came in the large kalia

to Muifonua?
13. Why were the children's eyes glowing?
14. Did the children talk?
15. What did the children do every morning?
16. What house did 'Etumatupu'a ask Latou to built?
17. How long did the children beings stay at Muifonua?
18. Where do you think the children beings came from?
19. What name did latou and Mafanga gave their place at Muifonua?

About the author…..

Semisi Pule also known as Semisi Pule Pone Uses the name Semisi Pone for short. He was born and raised on the small island Kingdom of Tonga. He attended the local Longolongo Primary School and Tonga High School then Mt Albert Grammar School and Auckland University in New Zealand. He graduated in May, 1985 with a Bachelor of Science.

He was offered a job with the Ministry of Agriculture, Fisheries and Forests in June 1985 where he carried out research on Kava, Vanilla and Squash Pumpkin viruses. He was given a scholarship by the Government of Germany to do a Master of Science degree which he completed in 1989.

In April 1992 he joined the University of the South Pacific, Institute for Research, Extension and Training in Agriculture, Alafua Campus in Samoa as a Fellow in Tissue Culture.

He was offered the position of Plant Protection Advisor and co-ordinator of the Plant Protection Service, South Pacific Commission, Suva, Fiji in May 1993. During his time with SPC he co-ordinated more than $NZ30 million worth of projects and managed a $NZ5 million project. He was also the Chief Executive of the newly established Pacific Plant Protection Organization and represented the Pacific region in the United Nations Food and Agriculture Organization Expert Panel on Biosecurity/Phytosanitary Measures and the Technical Consultation among Regional Plant Protection Organizations in Rome every year.

He migrated with his family to New Zealand in June 1996 where he was involved with many industries. He started writing in 2009 and has published more than 200 books and ebooks in amazon.com and blurb.com.

He also manage a small contracts business.

www.ingramcontent.com/pod-product-compliance
Lightning Source LLC
Chambersburg PA
CBHW060222050426
42446CB00013B/3145